THIS BOOK IS DEDICATED TO DR. PATRICIA BLOUNT- BROWN,
MY ORIGINAL CANCER WARRIOR AND TO MODERN DAY
WARRIOR MOMMIES,
AUNT GWEN, TRICIA & STEPHANIE,
I LOVE YOU!

*To my relief,
Mommy said,
"Baby, don't worry,
Just know that I've got this."
I know exactly what to do!
I will become a Cancer Warrior!
It's an elite special crew.*

She said,
"People all over the world get cancer,
And no one really knows why."

"Mommy is going to fight her cancer
So there's no need to cry."

So dry your eyes
And let's begin.
I'll explain what cancer is...

Cancer happens when good cells go bad,
The bad ones never stay in place.
They tend to swell in clusters
and invade the organ's space.

My body is the battlefield
Because cancer doesn't like to play nice.
My special warrior cells, with the help from medicine and doctors
Will make the bad cancer cells think twice!
They'll chase the cancer
Straight out of there,
Because cancer must be stopped!

Then mommy got serious and looked me in the eye,
She said,
"Cancer has to be treated swiftly"!
...like in the blink of an eye.

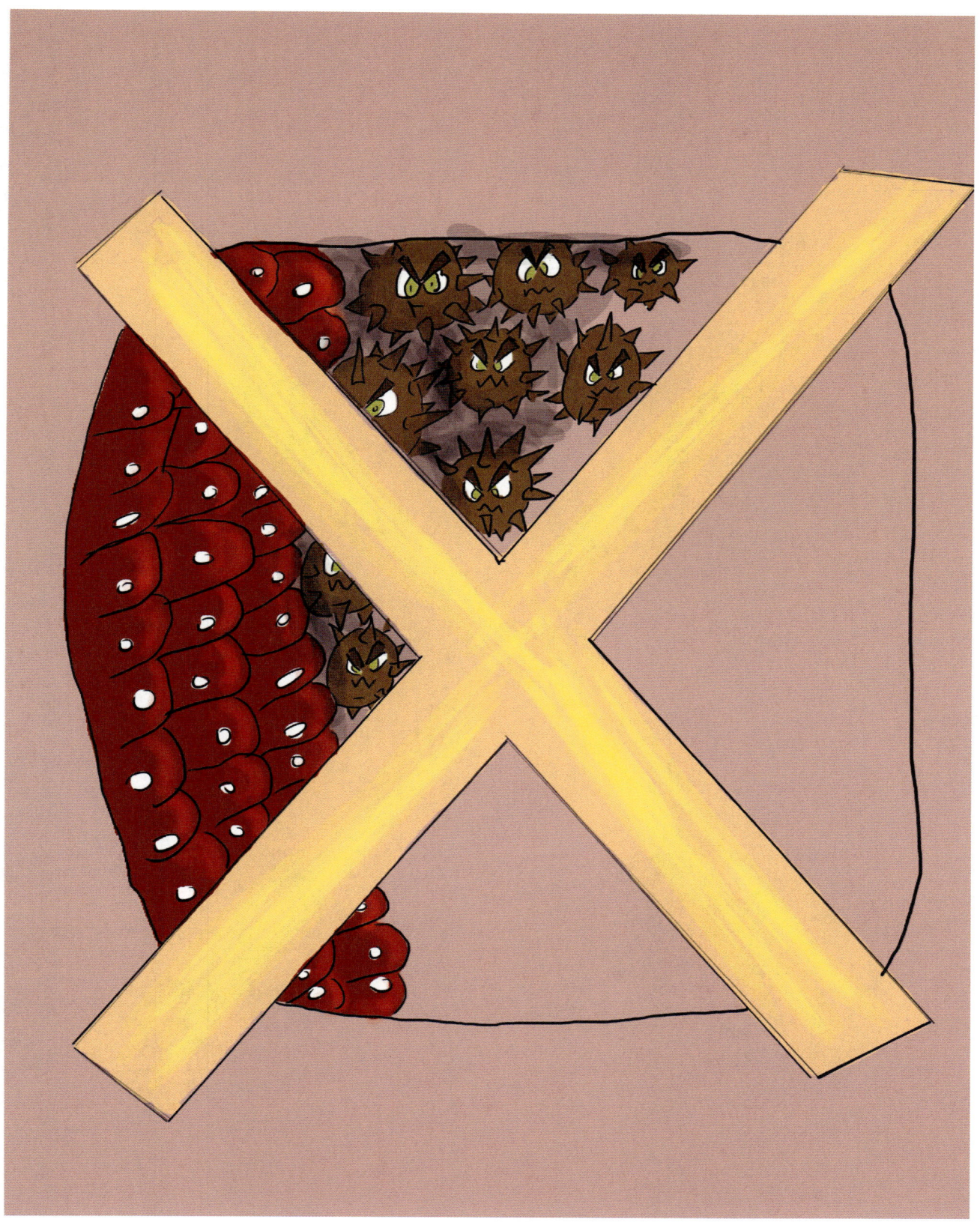

Because cancer cells tend to multiply quickly
Taking over places it should not.
I have to get it out of me, because it can't stay in its current spot!

I want the strongest possible.
Mommy warrior,
So that she can win!

Next, mommy warrior will need
a lot of strength
From good and healthy food.
Making sure she eats
Fruits and veggies
Is something I can do!

Last but not least,
And certainly most important.

Making sure I wash my hands

And clean any
Nasty, sniffly snotty noses.

*My mommy's fighting a battle
Deep within
This is a battle, I want her to win!*

*She has no time for
Colds and germs
I must do my part
To help her remain prepared.*

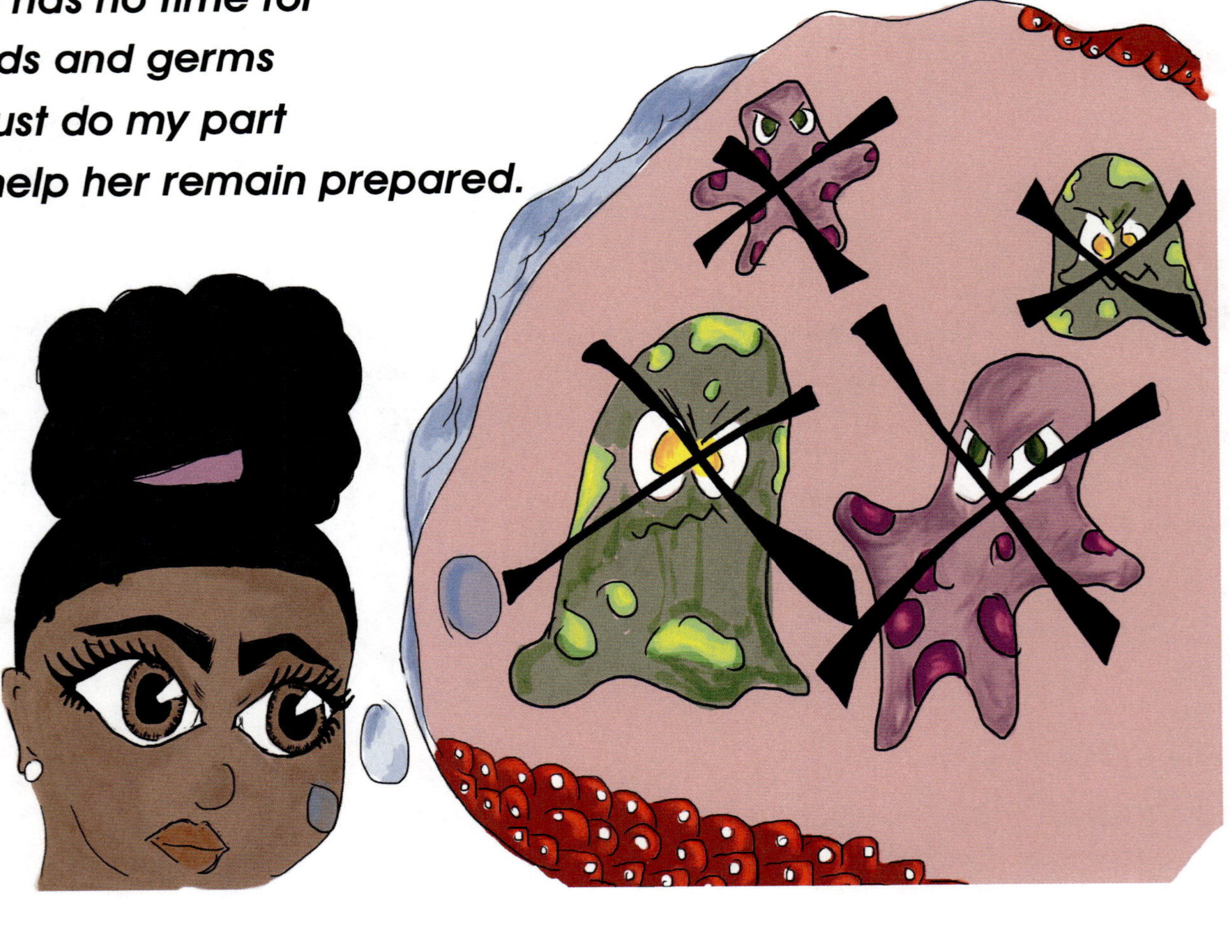

My brain wandered off,
Thinking about how I can help.

Then she cleared her throat,
To regain my attention.
She said,
"Her appearance might change a little.
I didn't want to forget to mention."

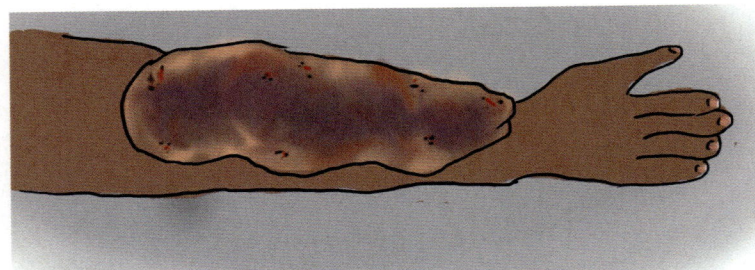

"My skin might turn red in spots,
And be swollen and bruised."

"I might even cut my hair
And rock a short fabulous do."

"I may even be **bold**,
And go bald,

There's no telling what I'll do!"

**And finally,
she said,
" I want to make something perfectly clear,
When a warrior goes to battle, sometimes they win, sometime they lose."**

She said,
"It's all about the journey spent and sisters gained along the way.
For each warrior's life is special and a testament of values like:
Confidence,
Strength,
Discipline and Bravery!"

Of all the things she said to me
And how fierce she must really be.
A cancer warrior,
Through and through
Brave
Powerful
And True!

Note from the Author

"A lump," is what she said when I went for my routine appointment with my OB-GYN and my first thoughts were, is history going to repeat itself. My mother was diagnosed with Stage 4 Breast Cancer at 31, and it looked like I was headed for the same diagnosis at age 33. That's when my search began for the perfect book to help break my news to my daughters, who were 5 and 1 at the time. I was looking for a book that spoke to me and reflected my mother's character. I couldn't find it.

After receiving a negative diagnosis, I had time to reflect on all the women that I know that are going through cancer, and I decided to write the book I couldn't find. I started with the premise that my mother was not a superhero. As a fans of superheroes, most of them don't die and have special powers they use to overcome obstacles. It made me feel left out like there was something wrong with my mother's fight. The inspiration for this book was the fictional African Warrior women of Wakanda. There was something that resonated with my soul about these characters. When my mother fought cancer, she did it in a fashion that resembled the fight of these characters. These warriors women fought with courage, have battle scars, stood tall throughout their many battles and obstacles, supported each other, and occasionally shaved their heads! No extraordinary powers outside of will-power and perseverance!

I wrote this story to help families introduce the topic of cancer to their children, to be a repeated bedtime story of strength, perseverance, and empowerment. This story is to be a reminder that everyone can do their part to help, to honor all cancer warriors on their journey and the families that go on the trip with them. I wanted my daughters to see themselves reflected in this story, see my strength, and honor the perseverance of their Grandmother, who was and will forever be a Cancer Warrior!

Alyss Blount

Made in the USA
Coppell, TX
29 September 2021